Copyright Kim Sorgius 2015.

ALL RIGHTS RESERVED. This book contains material protected under International and Federal Copyright Laws and Treaties. Any unauthorized reprint or use of this material is prohibited. No part of this book may be reproduced or transmitted in any form or by any means, electronic or mechanical, including photocopying, recording, or by any information storage and retrieval system without express written permission from the author / publisher.

Unless otherwise indicated, all Scripture quotations are from The Holy Bible, English Standard Version® (ESV®), copyright © 2001 by Crossway, a publishing ministry of Good News Publishers. Used by permission. All rights reserved.

All Scripture quotations marked (KJV) are from The Holy Bible, King James Version. Public Domain.

The purchaser of this ebook has permission to print unlimited copies of the ebook text and journal for immediate family use only. For any group consisting of more than one immediate family, each family is required to purchase a copy of this ebook.

Table of Contents

PART I: INTRODUCTION
    Upside Down World
    Truth or Lies?
    Where Am I Now?
    A Real Look at Poverty
    What is Contentment?
    A Content Heart

PART II: LEARNING TO BE CONTENT WITH MYSELF
    My Appearance
    My Abilities
    My Rights
    My Place
    Review

PART III: LEARNING TO BE CONTENT IN ALL CIRCUMSTANCES
    My Family
    My School
    My Finances
    My Situation
    Review

PART IV: LEARNING TO BE CONTENT WITH MY THINGS
    My Food
    My Space
    My Possessions
    My Possessions (part 2)
    My Gifts
    Review

Introduction

Upside Down World

Whether you live in the United States or China, we are all living in the world God created. But what people don't always understand is that this is not exactly the WAY that God created it. Glance over Genesis 1 and record the number of times you see the word "good."

Using a thesaurus, list several synonyms for the word good.

Today, the word "good" is used to describe so many things that it doesn't seem all that impressive to us. But in this case, good means exactly what the dictionary says: possessing or displaying moral virtue, giving pleasure, satisfying. God made the earth 100% perfect. There was no death and no pain. Everything was in perfect harmony.

Draw how you imagine the world looked in Genesis 1.

A Content Heart | ©Not Consumed 2015

Sadly, the world didn't stay that way. You are probably familiar with the story of the fall in Genesis 3, but let's turn there together. After you read it, write a short summary of what happened to the world. (Don't just record what happened- look beyond that.)

_____

_____

_____

In our family, we sing a song about this tragic turn of events. The chorus says, "right side up, turned upside down" and that is exactly what happened. When man chose sin, God cursed that ground and nothing would ever be the same again. What was right, good, and holy would forever be wicked.

List some examples of sin and evil in the world today. Think about Genesis 3 as you answer.

_____   _____

_____   _____

_____   _____

_____

I want to remind you of that now, before we begin this study, because it's important for us to understand that God wants us to walk righteously (right side up) in a world that we cannot trust. We have an enemy who wants to trick us just like he did Adam and Eve and he often does this by appealing to our desire to be like those around us. As Christians, we may not be able to look at what someone around us is doing and decide that it is OK for us to do as well. In fact, that will often be the wrong answer. We must remember to make our choices based on God's Word and not what everyone else seems to be doing or thinking. I'm going to be reminding you of this a lot during this study, so you will know what I mean if I say, "Is your thinking turned right side up or upside down?"

PAUSE FOR PRAYER:
Before we leave our study today, set a timer and spend 5 minutes praying. Thank God for making the world and ask Him to show you how to walk righteously (right side up) instead of upside down.

A Content Heart | ©Not Consumed 2015

Truth or Lies?

Yesterday we talked about how the world became upside down. Let's start today by making sure we have the facts straight.

> **FACT:**
> The Word of the Lord is _____.
>
> His work is done in _____.
> (Psalm 33:4)

It's really important that we know and believe that God is truth. We need to remember that His truth is written for us in the Bible. We don't have to guess or wonder. The answer is always in God's Word. And best of all, God is always faithful to keep His promises.

How much truth does the enemy have? The Bible says none. That means absolutely not ONE word that he speaks is true. The Bible says that absolutely everything Satan whispers into our ears is a lie.

Have you ever told a lie? I know you have and I imagine you can remember what it felt like when your parents didn't believe you. In fact, you probably kept on lying in hopes that you would convince them to believe you, didn't you?

> **FACT:**
> Satan is the father of _____.
>
> In him there is _____ truth. (John 8:44)

This is exactly what Satan does to us. His primary goal and desire is to get us to believe him. He's not going to stop with just lying to us. He will use any tactic he can to convince us that God's words aren't really true. Just like he did with Adam and Eve. He doesn't give up without a fight!

Read 1 Peter 5:8 and write it below.

_____

_____

_____

There is no question that the devil wants to keep us from loving God and walking righteously with Him. But we need to be careful about putting all the blame on him. When we sin, we shouldn't be like Adam and Eve and start pointing fingers. Saying "the devil made me do it" is only partly true. He might have tricked or tempted us, but we always have a choice as to whether or not we will fall into that trap.

Have you listened to the enemy recently and found yourself disobeying God, your parents, or other adults? Write what happened here.

_____

_____

_____

A Content Heart | ©Not Consumed 2015

So let's review. We know that Satan wants to trick us and lie to us. We know that we will be responsible for our choices just like Adam and Eve were in the garden. So, what can we do to help ourselves stay on the right path?

KNOW GOD'S WORD

The first thing we will need to do is know God's Word. Remember what Jesus did when He was tempted by Satan in the desert? Read Matthew 4:1-11. Every time He was tempted, Jesus answered the devil with what?

___

Read Hebrews 4:12. Write how God's Word can help us.

___

Of course, if we are going to use God's Word to help us fight the enemy, we will need to know it. Write Psalm 119:11 here.

___

LEARN TO DISCERN LIES

Knowing God's Word will greatly help us with this next step. We must take everything we hear and compare it to what God says. Whether it's coming from a slithery snake or a popular girl at school, we must be very careful to believe only what God says about a matter. If not, we will find ourselves in a heap of trouble just like Adam and Eve did.

Read Colossians 2:8. This verse has a few difficult words in it, so take it to your parents have them help you understand what it means. Write what you learn below.

___

REPLACE LIES WITH TRUTH

Once we know that something is a lie, we need to replace that lie with truth. If we keep thinking on it, our hearts will be more and more tempted to sin. Let's read Romans 12:2. What is the secret to not believing the lies?

___

We are to "renew" our minds which means that we will need to be reading and memorizing God's Word as often as possible. If we do, we will be ready when the world throws a lie our way.

PAUSE FOR PRAYER:
Pray and ask God to help you learn to recognize the lies of the world and to fill your mind with God's truth.

A Content Heart | ©Not Consumed 2015

Where Am I Now?

Today let's take a little "quiz" to see just where your heart is BEFORE we begin the study. Now be honest with yourself. Pick the answer that you really would do if no one was looking. There is no room for growth if you aren't honest with yourself!

1. I like the way I look and wouldn't change anything. ◯ YES ◯ NO
2. Our house is the best. ◯ YES ◯ NO
3. My parents work hard to give us what we need. ◯ YES ◯ NO
4. I have all the toys I really need. ◯ YES ◯ NO
5. I feel thankful for any food we have for dinner, even if I don't like it. ◯ YES ◯ NO
6. When things don't go my way, I feel thankful. ◯ YES ◯ NO
7. It's ok if I'm not the best at some things. ◯ YES ◯ NO
8. I have all the clothes I need and I like them. ◯ YES ◯ NO
9. I love the town we live in. The weather is perfect. ◯ YES ◯ NO
10. My brothers and sisters are a blessing to me. ◯ YES ◯ NO

Give yourself one point for every YES you checked.
Write your score here. _____

Now let's do a few more.

11. I wish we lived in a better neighborhood. ◯ YES ◯ NO
12. I wish I didn't have to go to school or do schoolwork. ◯ YES ◯ NO
13. My friends have toys or things I wish I had. ◯ YES ◯ NO
14. I wish my parents would let me do the things my friends' parents let them do. ◯ YES ◯ NO
15. I'd be happier if I had my own room. ◯ YES ◯ NO
16. Sometimes I worry that things won't work out. ◯ YES ◯ NO
17. I wish I was a little taller or that my hair was different. ◯ YES ◯ NO
18. I wish I could trade siblings with someone else. ◯ YES ◯ NO
19. If I don't like something, I will find a way to get my way. ◯ YES ◯ NO
20. I wish my life was easier. ◯ YES ◯ NO

Give yourself one point for every NO that you checked this time.
Write your score here. _____

A Content Heart | ©Not Consumed 2015

Congratulations. You've finished the quiz. Now add your two scores together and let's see how you did. Circle the category that you fit in now.

0-5 POINTS
I'm afraid your heart is rather discontent. You're not happy with anything that God has given you. But don't fret, that means you have the most room for growth. Hang onto your hat, it's going to be a wild ride!

6-10 POINTS
There are a few things in your life that you are content with, but there is a lot of room for growth. I can't wait to see how much you learn in this study!

11-15 POINTS
You seem to be fairly content with what God has given you. Let's work on those last few places over the next few weeks. It's going to grow and change you in ways you never imagined!

16-20 POINTS
You're at the top of the class. If you've been honest with yourself, then you are doing a pretty good job with this contentment thing. But let me remind you that there is always room to grow. Even the strongest Christians are constantly looking for ways to grow. It might be a bit harder for you to find, but pay close attention during this study and you'll find ways to improve!

I'm really excited to be on this journey together. It is my prayer that you will study Scripture that will change your life over the next few weeks. If you truly read it and ask God to change your heart, you will see a difference!

PAUSE FOR PRAYER:
Take a few minutes today and talk to God about what you learned while taking this quiz. Are you excited to learn more about being content or are you grumpy and complaining? Ask Him to help you be ready to listen and grow as He teaches you.

A Content Heart | ©Not Consumed 2015

A Real Look at Poverty

When I was a kid my mom always said that I needed to eat my food because there were starving kids in Ethiopia. I am going to be honest with you, I thought that was totally dumb. First, I didn't even know where Ethiopia was and as far as I knew, no one was starving. Second, how will it help starving kids in Africa if I eat all of my food?

The truth is- I was very misinformed. In fact, I was dead wrong on all accounts. Don't let that be you. Look at the chart on the right and fill in the information.

Almost half of the kids living in the world today do not have these three things:

1. _____

2. _____

3. _____

_____ in _____ people will go to bed hungry tonight. Draw 7 people below and color only the people who get to eat tonight.

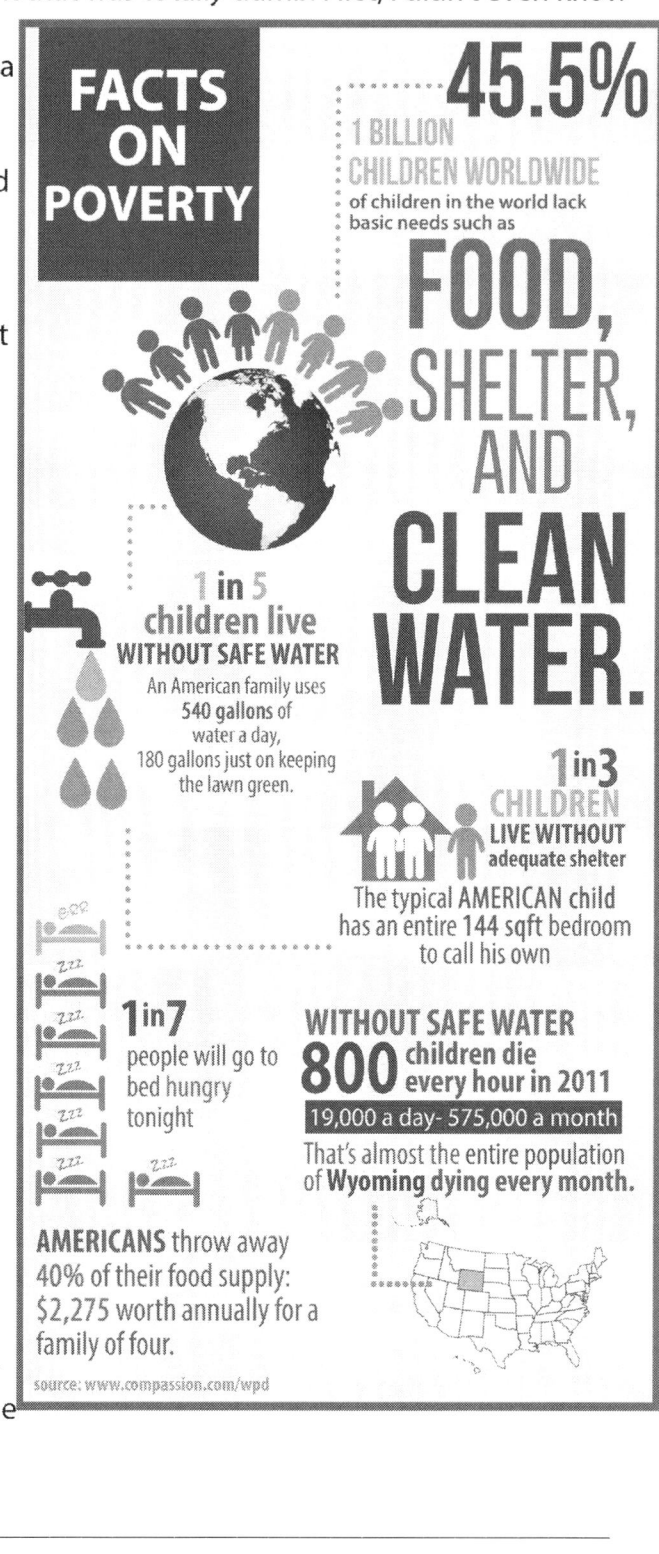

_____ in _____ children do not have any kind of shelter. That means they have no house, no apartment, no hut, no tent, nothing. Draw 2 houses below with children inside and one child without a house.

_____ children die every hour because they don't have this basic thing along with the lack of medical care. How does this make you feel?

_____

_____

A Content Heart | ©Not Consumed 2015

Grocery List

Watch this video: https://youtu.be/l1Y2wVucQEY

Half of the world lives in poverty, defined as less than $2 per day. Can you even imagine what it would be like to have only $2 per day to live? Let's do some field study. Go to the grocery store or look through a grocery ad with your parents. Make a list of the things you could buy if you had only $2 per day for the whole week. Remember, that's $14 total!

Was it difficult to do that? I know it was. $14 won't buy you much in the store if you want to eat for a week, but it's worse than that. Don't forget that they ONLY have that $14 for the week. That money has to be divided between food, water, housing, clothes, and anything else the family may need.

So let me ask you a question. How many toys do you think a child living on only $2 per day will have?

_____

Every single person who will read this Bible study is absolutely rich in comparison to half of the people in the world. You have so much more than $2 per day. Just look at all you have.

Put a check mark in the right box.

Do you have a bed to sleep on?	○ YES	○ NO
Do you have a house to sleep in?	○ YES	○ NO
Do you have a room with a roof, doors, and windows?	○ YES	○ NO
Do you have a pillow to sleep on?	○ YES	○ NO
Do you have clean water to drink?	○ YES	○ NO
Do you have food to eat?	○ YES	○ NO
Do you own a pair of shoes?	○ YES	○ NO
Do you have more than one outfit?	○ YES	○ NO
Do you have at least one toy?	○ YES	○ NO
Do you go to school?	○ YES	○ NO

If you answered yes to ANY of those questions, you are RICH! Yes, it's true. But I need to say it one more time so you really understand. HALF of the children in the world do not have any of the things I put on that list. We are going to talk much more about this, but for now let's end by talking to God.

PAUSE FOR PRAYER: What has God shown you through this lesson? How do you feel after reading this? Open your heart to God through prayer.

A Content Heart | ©Not Consumed 2015

What is Contentment?

I hope you are still thinking about the boys and girls that we talked about yesterday. I also hope you are feeling pretty thankful for a clean, quiet, and safe place to sleep last night. And for the fact that you aren't truly starving right now. (Even if you are doing this right before your next meal- that is not the kind of starving I mean!)

I don't know about you, but I can't stop thinking about all of the children and families all over the world who truly have great needs. I can't stop thinking about them because I know that I am guilty of being unhappy with what God has given me. Have you been feeling the same way?

Don't worry. These feelings are exactly what we are going to learn about in this Bible study. We are going to discover what God has to say about the topic of contentment, what it means for us, and how our lives should be changed. So let's get started!

Before we can really understand what all of this is about, we need to get out the dictionary and learn what a few of these words mean. Let's start with the word contentment.

THE WORLD'S DICTIONARY SAYS:
the feeling of peaceful happiness

Remember a few days ago when I mentioned that the world has a very tricky way of making us think they are right? Just look at those two definitions. They sound almost the same, but if you look closely there is a HUGE difference. Notice in the dictionary definition that contentment is a feeling. Circle that word in the definition. We usually say that we feel with our heart. Now notice which part of the body the Bible mentions. Circle it.

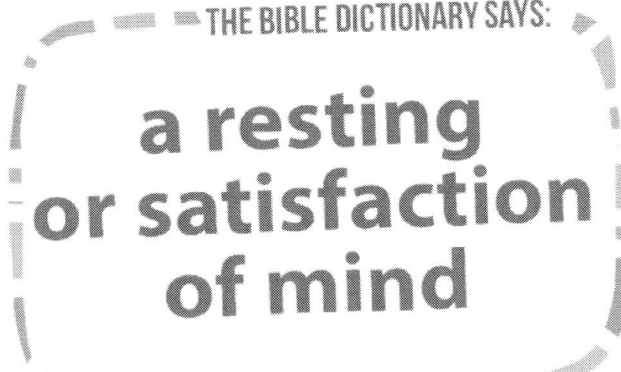

THE BIBLE DICTIONARY SAYS:
a resting or satisfaction of mind

Do you see the difference? We may never FEEL content, but the Bible says we can make up our minds to BE content. That's pretty awesome news.

Let's take a quick look at what the Bible says about being content. (We will come back to some of these later, so don't worry if it seems like we are going too fast.) Write what you find about contentment from each verse.

Philippians 4:12-13 _____

Hebrews 13:5 _____

1 Timothy 6:6-8 _____

A Content Heart | ©Not Consumed 2015

There are two other words that I think we need to clearly define as well: happiness and joy. These words are used a lot by people in our culture. Well, at least one of them is. Can you guess which one?
_____

Most people have one goal in life- to be happy. They want to do, have, and be whatever it takes to be happy. Of course there is a problem with that. Happiness is a feeling that is directly a result of the things that are happening in your life. Happiness might be caused by a new outfit, a sunny day, a new friend, or getting the lead role in the church play.

The trouble with happiness is that we can't always have these things. While most of them are probably good things, God doesn't always give them to us. So what happens when our friend moves away, we don't make the soccer team, or there's no money for a new outfit? Well, we don't feel happy do we?

	THE WORLD'S DICTIONARY SAYS:	THE BIBLE DICTIONARY SAYS:
joy	a feeling of great pleasure	glad or welcomed expectation of good
happiness	feeling pleasure	lucky, fortunate, successful

NAME SOME THINGS THAT MAKE YOU FEEL HAPPY

But that's OK. Not feeling happy isn't a sin. It's actually normal. The Bible doesn't tell us that we have to feel happy. But it does tell us that we need to have joy. Look back up at the definitions for the word joy. The Bible definition probably seems a little strange to you. Let me explain. When we have joy, it is a gladness or a welcoming of what we are expecting God to do. It really doesn't have anything to do with our actual circumstances (or situation). For example, we can still have joy when we don't make the soccer team because we know and trust that God is good and that He has perfect plans.

Think of it like this. Happiness comes from our circumstances. Joy comes from our faith in God.

It's joy that brings a smile to our face no matter what is happening in our life!

PAUSE FOR PRAYER:
Let's end today by reading and meditating on Philippians 4:4-8. Read it several times out loud and then make those words the prayer of your heart!

A Content Heart

We are going to be spending the rest of this study learning how to have a content heart. We will look in detail at many things that are a big problem in life today. Some may not be as big of a deal for you personally and others may be giant problems. If you really want to be content with what God has given you, you'll need to be honest with yourself about this because no one else can do it for you!

So let's begin by learning what a truly content heart looks like.

A content heart is always thankful.
Read 1 Thessalonians 5:18 and write it below. Circle the word that tells you WHEN to be thankful.

_____

_____

There are so many other verses on this topic, but this one makes it pretty clear, doesn't it? God wants us to be thankful no matter what happens. We can be thankful for even the bad things because we know that God is always good and that He always works for our good.

Oh, and this also means no more complaining, okie dokie? If you think it's ok to complain, stop right now and read Philippians 2:14.

TEN THINGS I HAVE TO BE THANKFUL FOR:
1. _____
2. _____
3. _____
4. _____
5. _____
6. _____
7. _____
8. _____
9. _____
10. _____

A content heart rejoices with others.
When someone around you has great news, what is your response? I know it's not always the right one, but let's look at what the right one should be. Write what you learn from these verses.

Romans 12:15 _____

_____

James 3:14-16 _____

_____

A Content Heart | ©Not Consumed 2015

Contentment means not being jealous or selfishly wanting something for yourself. I hate to tell you this, but life is not always fair. In fact, it's almost never fair. But that is a good thing because don't you remember what "fair" punishment you would have coming to you if God didn't send Jesus to wash away your sins? As a Christian, there is no room for the attitude that says, "That's not fair." It's time to rejoice with the other person!

Draw or write about a recent time when something good happened to a friend or family member.

A content heart serves first.

We've established that we can't be jealous, but there's a bit more to it. A content heart truly seeks to serve the needs of others BEFORE it serves the needs of itself. Read Philippians 2:3 and write it below.

_____

_____

Circle the words in the verse that you think are the hardest for you. This is a hard one, isn't it? There's no doubt that this is one of the verses in the Bible that most people want to skip over. The world says we should "take care of ourselves first" and it makes no room for anyone who stands in our way. But God has very different priorities. I can't wait to dig in to this one more later.

PAUSE FOR PRAYER:
Review each of the 3 markers of a truly content heart. Ask God to give you the desire to be truly content!

A Content Heart | ©Not Consumed 2015

TIME TO REFLECT

Learning to be Content with Myself

My Appearance

The first area of your life we are going to tackle is being content with yourself. Starting here will help us lay a good foundation for the next two topics. You may feel like you are pretty happy with yourself overall, but I challenge you to take this section seriously, as it's likely a few lies have snuck into your beliefs without you even realizing it!

Describe your physical appearance (hair color, eye color, height, etc.). How do you feel about the way you look?

_____

_____

_____

THE LIE: I am not good enough the way God made me.

This lie sneaks in to almost all of our hearts in one way or another. We start believing that we are not good enough physically. Perhaps we don't like our hair color or we want it to be curly instead of straight. Maybe we'd rather be taller, thinner, more athletic. The list is never-ending.

This is not a new lie, but I think it's becoming an even bigger problem for people today. Everywhere we go there are life-sized posters of what the world sees as "beautiful." The world looks at physical appearance to determine the worth of a person. This would include everything from hair color, eye color, height, weight, skin color, type of hair, and so much more.

Read 1 Samuel 16:7. What does the Lord use as a measure to choose someone for a task?

_____

_____

In case you don't recognize this passage, let me give you a little background. This is when Samuel was looking for a king for Israel. It's surprising to think that God was looking past things like height and strength. Aren't kings supposed to be strong? The answer is obvious. Yes, they are supposed to be strong. Strong in the Lord. It's their faith that God is after. He looks on us not like the rest of the world, who sees only the outside. He looks at our hearts.

After many years of wishing that my own physical appearance was different in some way, here's one thing I can promise you. God gave you what he gave you. You can wish it was different. You can color it different. You can hide it. But you can't change it. If you have freckles- you will always have freckles. If you are shorter than average- you will always be short.

We can't change this fact, but there is something much more important to consider. Should we even WANT to change how God made us? (Don't answer yet.) Read these verses and write what you learn.

Genesis 1:27 _____

Ephesians 2:10 _____

Psalm 139:13-14 _____

Matthew 10:29-31 _____

1 Peter 2:9 _____

A Content Heart | ©Not Consumed 2015

Hmm. Feeling a little guilty about what you were thinking about yourself when this lesson started? _____

How about the question I asked before. Do you think it's ok to want to change the way God made you?

God made you exactly the way He wanted you. You're perfect. Even if your nose is bigger than you'd like or your freckles make you feel like someone will come along and connect the dots any day now. (True story- yes, I have freckles.)

THE TRUTH:
I am perfectly and wonderfully made in the image of a magnificent and holy God.

We must remember that God does NOT make mistakes. He's perfect. Read Matthew 5:48 and write it below.

_____

_____

If God is perfect and He created you, then He did it exactly how He wanted you to be. Does that make sense? It's time we push out the lies of the world and find true contentment with ourselves exactly how God made us. It's not ok for us to be unhappy with the way God made us. It's not ok to want to change it. Your nose, your freckles, your height, your big toe... all of it was perfectly made by a loving God.

I AM...

_____

_____

_____

A content heart is always thankful! So, let's change our thinking right now. Write a new description of your physical appearance. Be sure to use words that God would use to describe you. (Like wonderfully made, perfect, created in His image, etc.)

By the way, just in case you don't know, all of the people you see on TV, in magazines, or in advertisements for stores are completely fake. What we see is their absolute best plus hours of make-up, fancy lights, and even photoshopping that makes them look way different than they actually do.

It's important for us to know the "enemy" we face. Even if we don't think we want to be like these "famous" people we see, many of our friends do and that desire will indeed rub off on us if we aren't careful. In fact, we might go after looking a certain way not even realizing that we are seeking to follow the world.

PAUSE FOR PRAYER:
Pray and ask God to help you to love the way you look just as much as He does. Remember, just because God wants you to love the way He made you doesn't make it super easy to do. You may need to spend a lot of time in prayer and reminding yourself of the truth!

A Content Heart | ©Not Consumed 2015

My Abilities

Write yesterday's truth about your appearance in the box.

Besides our physical appearance, there is one more thing about ourselves that we are often not content with: our gifts. No, I don't mean the stuff you find under the tree at Christmas. I'm talking about the gifts that God has chosen for you. Before I share too much, list below the things you think you are good at. Also list the things you wish you were good at and/or the things that you are not good at.

I'M GOOD AT...	I'M NOT GOOD AT...	I WISH I WAS GOOD AT...

Before you started this study, did you know that God chose very specific and unique gifts for you? _____. Let's take a look at a few verses so we can see exactly what God had in mind. Write what you find.

Romans 12:6 _____

_____

1 Peter 4:10 _____

_____

Another very helpful passage is 1 Corinthians 12:4-31. Read it carefully and write what you think the passage means.

_____

_____

_____

To put it simply, there are many different ways that God uses His children. As the passage says, each of us plays a part. There may be many "eyes" but there will also need to be hands, feet, and noses. This is why some people are good at soccer and other people are good at piano. Can you imagine if everyone was good at soccer and no one was good at piano? Well, at the very least, we wouldn't have music to sing on Sunday mornings!

A Content Heart | ©Not Consumed 2015

I am explaining this to you in a pretty simple way, but I want you to understand that this is actually a very big thing. God intentionally gave you gifts that He wants you to use to serve Him. You probably don't even know what most of them are yet! Some can be talents like athletic ability to play soccer or musical ability to play the piano. Others may be more difficult to see such as being good at encouraging others or being a good teacher.

Whatever they are, we need to see them the same way we see our physical appearance. They are gifts. We should be thankful both for what we have and what we don't have, instead of wishing it was different.

Remember, time spent wishing God made you differently is time spent NOT trusting Him. We don't want to be guilty of that.

PAUSE FOR PRAYER: Let's stop right here and ask God to help us be thankful for the things that we are good at and to help us to stop desiring the talents or gifts that others have.

By the way, there's one thing I don't want you to get confused about. There is a big difference between praying that God will help you to pass your math test and feeling jealous that it's so easy for your sister. Let's look at one passage about this. Read 2 Corinthians 12:8-10.

What does God do with our weaknesses?

_____

_____

I hope you can read those verses and see how God uses the things that are hard for us to teach us, grow us, and strengthen our faith. There have been many hard things in my life that I never could have done without God's help. One of those things was a college math class. It wouldn't have been right for me to give up and say, "Well, I'm no good at math." The class was required for graduation. So I had to endure.

You will face many things like this in your life. Know that God will use your weaknesses (the things you aren't so good at) to teach you and to grow your faith. I know it's hard to look forward to that, but we should! It's these kinds of lessons in life that really change who we are and make us even better at using the gifts God gave us!

What things are you struggling with right now? What weaknesses do you need to ask God to help you with?

_____

_____

_____

_____

A Content Heart | ©Not Consumed 2015

My Rights

Perhaps you did not have a big problem with the last two lessons. If so, this one might be one that needs your attention. You see, once we begin to trust God's goodness and believe we are wonderfully made, both physically and in giftedness, sometimes that can go to our head. In fact, sometimes we can become so content with who we are that we forget God has also called us to be humble. That lack of humilty it at the root of our next two problems.

When I was a kid, a popular fast-food restaurant came out with a jingle that promised you could "have it your way." Not that it's a bad idea to ask for your burger with no onions, but this kind of mindset can go all wrong very quickly, especially when you want things your way at any cost.

Let's say the fast food joint puts onions on your burger anyway. What will you do? Will it be ok to go up and punch the cashier? Should you open the burger and splatter it all over the counter in a fit of rage? Some people do respond this way, but Christians cannot.

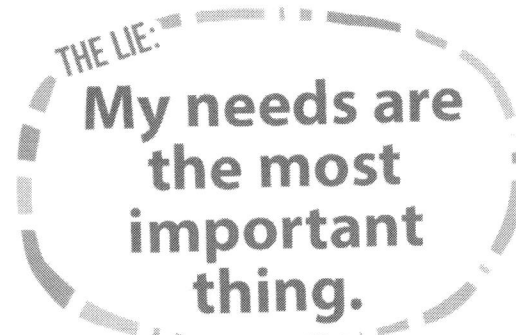

THE LIE: My needs are the most important thing.

Let's read Philippians 2:4 and see how God would handle the situation. Record what you think on the lines.

_____

_____

_____

What if the guy who was making your burger forgot? Maybe he was thinking about his mom being sick and not having enough money for the doctor. That doesn't make it right for him to fail to follow the instructions, but it should fill us with compassion for him. The truth is, we don't know why things don't go our way sometimes. We need to be careful that we don't put our need for silly things (like no onions) above the deeper needs of those around us (like compassion and salvation).

THE TRUTH: The needs of other people are just as important as my needs.

Let's make it a little more personal. If your sister gets the biggest cookie, what will you do? If your brother breaks your newest toy, how will you handle it?

These are big issues in our lives and they can be the cause of great sin. Think about the attitude behind your answers to the questions above. Are you mad about the cookie because you think YOU deserve the biggest cookie? Are you mad about the toy because it was YOURS and how dare he even touch it?

A Content Heart | ©Not Consumed 2015

This kind of thinking is a dangerous trap. It's very wrong, but many Christians can't even see why because they have believed the lie that their needs are more important than the needs of others. In fact, many people believe that they deserve to be happy no matter what happens to the other person. This isn't what God said in Philippians 2:4, is it?

Let's do a little activity to help us keep our thinking straight. Take a yellow crayon and highlight each of the things below that you would enjoy having. (Just color the words yellow.)

- The last piece of cake
- New bike
- Special treat
- Trip to an amusement park
- Nice outfit
- A solo in the church play
- My own room
- Stay up 1 hour later than bedtime
- $5 bill
- Own iPad or phone

Do you think there is anything bad or wrong about any of the things on the list? I'll give you a hint: no. There really is nothing wrong with wanting your own room or wanting to sing a solo in the church play. BUT- there is something else we need to consider. Let's say that if you get something on the list then no one else does. That means no one gets cake, a bike, the solo, $5, or to stay up late. Seem ok with you?

Maybe it does, but what happens when we flip the situation. Now everything you colored yellow is being given to one of your siblings and you can NOT have it at all. How do you feel?

_____

_____

_____

I know how you feel because I've been there many times. It's hard when someone else gets something we would enjoy having. It's even harder when that means we cannot have that thing. But we need to remember that if it wasn't wrong for you to have the thing, then it isn't wrong for them either. See what I mean? If your "rights" take away the rights of someone else, then they really aren't a good thing are they?

If there is only one piece of cake left, the options are pretty limited. Share it. Someone gets left out. Or throw it away. We could live our whole lives making everyone around us "throw away" special things because we can't have them, but there is no joy in that. True joy comes not from getting the last piece of cake, but from giving it. (More on this later).

PAUSE FOR PRAYER:
Ask God to show you how you are demanding your way and how you can stop. Ask Him to show you how to be more considerate of the needs of others.

A Content Heart | ©Not Consumed 2015

My Place

Yesterday we talked about considering the needs of others just as much as we consider our needs. We learned not to demand our "rights" to have or be something, especially when it means that someone else will miss out or suffer. We have to learn to be ok with God allowing someone else to get the thing we desire. That's true contentment. But let's take it a step further.

If you put a piece of pie on the table, most people would never admit that they think they should be first. At least not out loud anyway. It's possible that most Christians even truly believe they don't need to have the first piece of pie. But this lie is much sneakier than the issue of pie.

Look at the list below and circle all the things you have done in the last few weeks.

- been first in line
- sat in the front seat
- tried for the most important role
- taken the first turn on the computer
- told mom about your day before others
- gone through the door first
- scored a soccer goal
- chose your snack first
- gotten to the car first
- finished school work first
- taken the first swing or slide at the playground
- taken the first bite
- given the answer to a question in class
- sat next to mom/dad

The world is convinced that we should take care of ourselves first. We are told to put our own needs above those of other people so we can have more, be more, and do more. If we are being honest with ourselves, there are probably more times this week that we have been "first" than we even put on the list. Even grown-ups face this situation at a traffic light or while in line at the grocery store. The truth is, our hearts desire to be first. We naturally think of ourselves first. But that doesn't make it right.

Read Matthew 23:11. What does God think about being first?

_____

_____

Hmm. Those are pretty strong words aren't they? I don't think we can support the view that we should put ourselves first with Scripture can we? The truth is, God has no intention at all for us to ever be first. He wants us to have a heart that is willing to put others above ourselves. Let's see what we can learn from a few other verses.

1 Corinthians 10:24 _____

Philippians 2:3 _____

Hebrews 13:16 _____

A Content Heart | ©Not Consumed 2015

Let's look together at the example Jesus left us. Read John 13:3-5.

Where are Jesus and His disciples? _____

What did Jesus do for the disciples? _____

Does this seem right to you? _____

Skip down to John 13:12-16. What does Jesus explain to them?

_____

_____

_____

THE TRUTH:
A Christian always serves others first.

Can you see the picture Jesus painted for us here? He was God in the flesh. He was the teacher, master, and leader of this group. It would have been normal and reverent for the disciples to wash His feet. But He didn't allow that. Instead, He washed theirs.

It doesn't come naturally to us, but it is exactly what we are called to do. Jesus gave us a very clear example.

He didn't race to the front of the line, take the best seat, or eat the first piece of bread. He also didn't ask others to treat Him special. Instead, He did something that would honor them.

Let's put this into practice. Think of 3 ways that you put yourself first recently. Then write how you could have served someone else instead. Try to be specific.

ME FIRST	THEM FIRST

PAUSE FOR PRAYER:
Pray and ask God to help you want to serve others more than yourself. Ask Him to help you find ways to step back and allow others to shine.

Review

PRACTICE THE TRUTH:
We hear the lies of the world every day. In fact, they are so common in our culture that we don't even realize we are hearing them. We must fight these lies by rehearsing or practicing the truth out loud to ourselves. Fill in the blanks and write these truths. Then practice saying them out loud 3 times.

THE TRUTH:
I am perfectly and wonderfully made in the image of a magnificent and holy God.

_____

_____

THE TRUTH:
The needs of other people are just as important as my needs.

_____

_____

_____

A Content Heart | ©Not Consumed 2015

5 Things My Siblings Need From Me This Week:

1. _____

2. _____

3. _____

4. _____

5. _____

THE TRUTH:
A Christian always serves others first.

_____

_____

Let's make a plan for how you can serve others this week. Ask your parents to show you a calendar of what is happening over the next several days. Then write an event, a person you will serve, and how you will serve them. Remember, this can be something simple like giving your seat to an older lady on a crowded bus, holding open the door, or letting someone else get water before you.

EVENT	PEOPLE TO SERVE	ACTION PLAN

PAUSE FOR PRAYER:
Ask God to show you opportunities where you can practice what you are learning. Ask Him to open your heart and help you to be willing!

A Content Heart | ©Not Consumed 2015

TIME TO REFLECT

Learning to be Content in All Circumstances

My Family

This week we are going to talk about being content in our circumstances. Let's write 1 Thessalonians 5:18 out again.

_____

_____

The word "circumstance" simply means the facts surrounding a situation. Let's take your family for example.

NAMES OF PEOPLE WHO LIVE IN YOUR HOME
_____
_____
_____

I have _____ sisters and _____ brothers.

Our house is _____
_____
_____

All of the things you listed above are your circumstances. They are the facts about your life right this minute. Circumstances can change, but you don't always get to choose how they change. For example, your parents might have another baby. Will you get to decide if it's a boy or a girl? Nope. They don't get to decide that either.

For the most part, God decides the details or circumstances of our lives, which is why it's important to understand what He wants us to do. Look back at the verse you wrote at the top. What does God want us to do?

_____

That's right. He wants us to give thanks. Even if we have a hard time getting along with our brother, wish we had a sister, or hate the new school we moved to, God has asked us to be thankful for it. Even if we are so sick that we can't get out of bed, our turtle died, or we don't have enough money for special treats, God still wants us to be thankful.

THE LIE: I should have a say over what happens in my life.

I know what you are thinking... *"but being thankful for ugly or unpleasant things in life is not easy."* Boy are you right about that! It is very hard to be thankful when you don't like the situation in your life, even for grown-ups. In fact, it's so hard that we've come up with some pretty tempting lies to believe about this topic.

Another way to say this is "I'm in control." We want to believe that this is true and we are often told that we are in control of our lives. This gets kinda tricky because in some ways our choices do determine what happens to us. But the truth is, sometimes we make a good choice and the outcome isn't what we had planned.

Has this ever happened to you? _____

_____

_____

A Content Heart | ©Not Consumed 2015

Read Psalm 115:3 and write it below.

_____

This verse makes me laugh. Wouldn't you like to be sitting up there in heaven doing whatever you please? I think we all would. But we would all fail miserably because we are not God. Not to mention, there are two really good reasons why we should let Him be in control.

Read Romans 8:28 for the first reason and write it below.

_____

_____

I hope you can see from that verse that it's for our benefit to have God in control of our lives. He is always working things for our good, even when it doesn't seem like it. Let's peek at Isaiah 14:24 for the second one. Write why you think this is good news.

_____

_____

THE TRUTH:
God is in control and He is always working things for my good.

I don't know about you, but if someone is going to be in control, I want it to be someone with enough power to actually accomplish what they planned. God has that power. In fact, He is the only one in the universe who does. Instead of constantly trying to take that power from Him, we should be incredibly thankful that we don't have to try to get everything right!

Now let's apply all of this to your family. Write some things down that have not made you happy in the past. What about your family do you wish was different?

_____

_____

It's time to put all of those thoughts behind you and trust God to be in control! Make a list right now of 9 reasons to be thankful for your family. Be creative!

_____   _____

_____   _____

_____   _____

_____

_____

PAUSE FOR PRAYER:
Pray and ask God to help you to step back and let Him be in control. Ask Him to help you be truly thankful for your family!

A Content Heart | ©Not Consumed 2015

My School

Speaking of not being in control, let's talk about school. Have you ever been guilty of not having a content heart when it comes to school? Check off all the things that are true below.

I have complained about school this week.	◯ YES	◯ NO
I don't like doing my school work.	◯ YES	◯ NO
I wish I didn't have to do some of the subjects.	◯ YES	◯ NO
I am not good at school.	◯ YES	◯ NO
If school were canceled my life would be easier.	◯ YES	◯ NO
School is such a waste of time.	◯ YES	◯ NO

If you checked yes in any of the boxes above, you've got a problem in this area. But don't worry. Knowing you have a problem is a good thing because you can work on it. If you didn't check yes and you lied, that's an even bigger problem. The truth is, you can't begin to work on yourself if you won't admit how you really feel.

Before I share with you, can you tell me why a bad attitude about school is not having a content heart?

_____

_____

_____

Of course, at the top of our list, we need to remember that a content heart is thankful in all circumstances. We also can look back at the first week and remember that God has gifted us with exactly what He wanted us to have. So maybe you struggle to understand math or perhaps it's difficult to read or spell. God didn't make a mistake. He knows this is hard for you and He intends to use this hard thing to help you grow.

Read James 1:2-4. Write 3 words that stand out to you based on what we have been learning. There are no wrong answers to that question, but I do hope you saw the word "JOY." What are we told to have joy about?

_____

_____

That seems so crazy doesn't it? When you struggle with math or don't read as easily as your friends, you are told to count it as joy. You are actually supposed to be thrilled! Is this what the world tells you to think?

A Content Heart | ©Not Consumed 2015

_____

_____

_____

It does go against what the world thinks and even what makes sense to a Christian. How can we be excited, thrilled, or have joy about something that is difficult, awful, or even devastating? Well, it's not the hard part or the trial that gives us the joy. We have to keep reading the verse.

Why should we have joy? (see verse 3) Because this testing of our faith produces _____.

Depending on which version of the Bible you are reading, that last word might be steadfastness, patience, or endurance. They basically mean the same thing. God uses hard things in our lives to teach us to be patient. Why? Look at verse 4 now for the rest of the answer. Write that whole verse below.

_____

_____

Circle the two words that describe what happens when God grows our faith through this patience (or steadfastness).

Isn't that awesome to think about? It doesn't even make sense to our minds. But it's true. So let's transfer it over to how we feel about that subject in school that gives us the most trouble. For me that would have been math, so I'll use it as an example in my sentence. You use whatever subject or situation about school you find to be the most difficult.

Me: Struggling in math helps me become more patient. God is using that to make me perfect and complete!

Now it's your turn. Write your sentence below. You can word it differently or just copy the same idea.

_____

_____

_____

_____

PAUSE FOR PRAYER:
Now it's time to look back at the boxes at the beginning of this lesson and ask God to forgive you for your attitude about any of the items that you checked "yes" for. Ask Him to help you to remember the verses that we learned today so that you can be truly thankful for even those subjects that are hard!

A Content Heart | ©Not Consumed 2015

My Finances

It's fairly easy to say we want to be content with what God has given us, but the truth is, actually feeling and acting content aren't nearly as easy! Have you ever stopped to think about why this is so hard? It really goes back to what we read a few days ago in Romans 8:28.

If we are going to be truly content, we will need to trust that God is in control and that He really is working all things for our good. This kind of trust gets pretty tricky when money gets tight. Has your family ever been in a situation where you could not afford to buy something you needed? I'm not talking about a trip to Disney or a new bike. I'm talking about things you really need like a place to live, food, even clothes.

Write about a time when your family was not able to afford something you needed.

_____
_____
_____

What did your family do about it? _____

_____

Let's find out what your Bible says about what you can and should do when you have a need that you can't afford to buy. Read Matthew 6:25-34. List the things God tells us NOT to worry about.

_____   _____   _____

        _____   _____

Not only does God tell us that we don't need to worry about all the basic needs of life (like food and clothes), He also tells us that He will take great care of us. Read that part of the Scripture again (v.26-29) and draw a picture that describes how God will take care of us.

A Content Heart | ©Not Consumed 2015

Let's consider one last part of this passage. What does God say is our part (v. 33)?

_____

_____

So now let's go back to that time when your family had a need for something that they couldn't afford. Maybe it was a car repair, a large electric bill, or even food. Did you respond by trusting God like it says to do in

Matthew 6:25-34? _____

Now that you know how to respond to this kind of problem, what will you do next time?

_____

_____

_____

This will come up again in your life. It may even be this week. Are you willing to trust God? Are you willing to help your family trust God? In 1 Timothy 4:12 it says that even young people like you can be an example to an older person. Wouldn't that be awesome?

Just remember that if you talk to an adult in a disrespectful way, it doesn't matter if what you said was true. You are still in the wrong. There is a way to remind your parents that we can trust God to help us with our money problems without being rude. So make sure you watch your attitude and tone if this comes up in your family. Your parents will be glad that you reminded them to trust God even when the situation seems very scary or frustrating.

PAUSE FOR PRAYER:
Pray and ask God to help you trust Him to provide for every single need you have. Confess the places where you haven't trusted Him and ask for forgiveness.

A Content Heart | ©Not Consumed 2015

My Situation

Today we are going to talk a little bit more about how to be content in every circumstance or situation. Have you noticed that there are times when you are not content with the situation? _____

Look back at the first day this week. What was the lie we sometimes believe about our situation? Write it here.

_____

We must remember that we are not in control. But there is one more lie that we often believe about our situation. Have you ever had a bad soccer game? Have you ever tried out for a part in a play only to have that part given to someone else? Have you ever gotten in trouble for something that you actually didn't do?

Or how about this one- have you ever known someone who died of cancer or another illness? I have. Actually, I have experienced all of these things and many others that didn't go my way. When this happens the first thing we want to shout is, "It's not FAIR!"

THE LIE: When things aren't going well for me, it's just NOT FAIR!

Have you ever thought or said that lie? Trust me, we all have! It just doesn't seem fair when things aren't going well for us. Christians are especially guilty of feeling this way. We can't understand why bad things happen to "good people." We try hard to love God and worship Him, but bad things still happen and we often don't have things the way we want them.

List some of the things in your life that just don't seem fair. They can be things that are still happening or things that happened in the past. Then write how you usually respond to this situation. Don't worry about the last column. We will fill it in later.

NOT FAIR	MY FIRST RESPONSE	MY NEW RESPONSE

Now let's look at the story of a man who didn't have a very fair life at all! Read Job 1. The Bible says that Job was a righteous man (Job 1:8). God allowed Satan to test Job to see if he would still love God and walk righteously with Him even if his life was not going well.

Satan killed Job's animals and servants (Job 1:14), then he killed his daughters and sons (v. 19).

A Content Heart | ©Not Consumed 2015

In Job 1:20 Job mourned over his family and the loss of his possessions, but notice in verses 21 and 22 what he did and said. Write them here.

_____

_____

It doesn't stop there. Satan continues to try and tempt Job to stop trusting God. (The whole book is a great book to read sometime when you have a few minutes.) After great trial Job does struggle with his situation, but he does the right thing. He takes his problems to God and God encourages him. One of my favorite verses in this book is Job 23:12. This was written in the middle of all his problems. What does Job say he will do?

_____

Those are pretty strong words, aren't they! Everything in Job's life was unfair. He hadn't done anything to cause this kind of trouble in his life. God was using Him for a greater purpose and Job didn't know it. We must remember that we are like Job. God may use some very hard things in our lives in order to accomplish His purpose.

In the end, what does God do for Job? (Read Job 42:10 and 12)

_____

_____

_____

THE TRUTH: God is always just.

We can trust God to be fair even when it doesn't seem fair to us. Remember how we learned that life is not all about our needs? A content heart has to consider that there are other people involved. In the story of Job, God was working in the lives of Satan, as well as Job's friends and family. And He worked an even stronger faith in Job's life.

I know it seems hard, but we must remember this truth when we start feeling like life isn't going our way or that something simply isn't fair. Look back at that list you made earlier. Now write in the third column and list reasons you can be thankful to God instead of feeling that something is unfair.

PAUSE FOR PRAYER:
Pray and ask God to help you stop feeling and saying "It's not fair." Ask Him to forgive you for all the times you did feel this way and then ask Him to help you remember to trust Him to be just (fair) as He promises He will be!

A Content Heart | ©Not Consumed 2015

Review

Before we review today, I want to talk about one thing we haven't had a chance to just yet: boredom. Have you told your parents that you were bored this week (maybe even today)?

_____

_____

Feeling "bored" is failing to show an attitude of contentment. It's forgetting that God has given you many talents, as well as everything that you need. Don't expect other people to entertain you with frivolous things. If you have time and don't know what to do, there are plenty of ways that you can grow! If all else fails, ask yourself these questions.

Have you...

Been creative?

Outside play?

Read a book?

Exercised for an hour?

Done something to help someone else?

Now let's review.

A CONTENT HEART   A CONTENT HEART   A CONTENT HEART

PRACTICE THE TRUTH:

We hear the lies of the world every day. In fact, they are so common in our culture that we don't even realize we are hearing them. We must fight these lies by rehearsing or practicing the truth out loud to ourselves. Fill in the blanks and write these truths. Then practice saying them out loud 3 times.

THE TRUTH:

God is in control and He is always working things for my good.

_____

_____

_____

A Content Heart | ©Not Consumed 2015

MAKE A LIST OF 5 GOOD THINGS THAT GOD HAS DONE FOR YOU THIS WEEK.

1.
2.
3.
4.
5.

THE TRUTH: God is always just.

Let's make a plan to pray for and help some people in your life who need you. In the first column, write the name of the person and the reason you chose them. Next, write how you are going to pray for them. In the final column, write how you will help them. Be as specific as possible. Then come back and check these off once you are done.

PERSON TO PRAY FOR	WHAT TO PRAY FOR THEM	HOW TO HELP THEM

PAUSE FOR PRAYER:
Ask God to show you opportunities where you can practice what you are learning. Ask Him to open your heart and help you to be willing!

A Content Heart | ©Not Consumed 2015

TIME TO REFLECT

4
Learning to be content with my things

My Food

So far in this study we have talked about being content with ourselves and our circumstances. Now we are going to talk about being content with "things." I know for sure that some of these lessons are going to be really hard for you. They are hard for me too. In fact, they are hard for most grown ups. But the faster you learn and the more content you become, the more joyful your heart will be! So let's get started!

Let's talk about your behavior at the dinner table. What happened last night when your parents served dinner? Did you smile, say thank you, and eat every bite or did you complain about anything?

___

Contentment with things starts with our food. Remember at the beginning of this study when we looked at how many children go to bed hungry every single night because they don't have enough to eat? That is a serious situation. Although we've learned that we shouldn't be anxious when our family is in a situation where money is so tight that we don't have enough to eat, I imagine most everyone who is reading this study is not in that situation right now. Chances are, your parents do have enough money to feed you.

So, are you thankful for just that? Or have you spent your time complaining about the foods you don't like?

___

One way to change your attitude at dinner is to look for the good. You might not like tomatoes, but what is on your plate that you do enjoy? Or perhaps it's not the food, but maybe you had a good conversation during dinner or you are just thankful for your mom who made the food. I want you to stop right now and write about last night's dinner. Tell everything you can about the dinner, but make sure you don't say anything negative at all.

"Our dinner was . . .
___
___
___

Now draw this glorious meal you had:

Doing this might seem a little silly to you, but I promise it's not. We need to focus on the good and stop focusing on the "bad" things in our lives. So mom served tomatoes and you don't like tomatoes; I'm positive the world won't end over that tragedy- know what I mean?

So step 1, start looking for the good things and thinking good things about the food you are served. Step 2, start trying new things. Yes I know you think it's gross. I understand that it looks funny. But I want you to really think about what would happen if your parents served that meal to a child in India who was living on the streets and hadn't eaten in days. Do you think that child would say, "Oh, I'm sorry but I don't like tomatoes." Absolutely NOT!

What do you think that child would say?_____

_____

Trust me. I really do understand that some foods just seem so hard to eat. I was a very picky eater growing up. But over the years, I've taught myself how to try new things and I've learned that MANY of the things that seemed awful are actually some of my favorites today.

So let's try something, ok? I want you to pick a food your family eats often that you pick out or don't eat. Write it on the line below.

_____

_____

Now, I want you to try that food 6 times. Yes, I said 6 times. I know that seems awful, but you won't like it the first few times because your mind has already convinced you that it doesn't taste good. Write how you feel each time you eat it and see what happens.

MY REACTION

○ _____
○ _____
○ _____
○ _____
○ _____
○ _____

PAUSE FOR PRAYER:
Ask God to help you be thankful for the food He has given you. Thank Him that these foods are good for your body. Then, ask Him to help you enjoy eating them.

A Content Heart | ©Not Consumed 2015

My Space

Let's start today by taking a little quiz to see just how content you are with your space. Answer each question below as honestly as possible. Remember, if you lie it might look good on paper, but it won't help you grow in your walk with Christ! So basically, you'll be wasting your time. What would be the point in that?

My room would be better if it was just a little bigger.	○ YES	○ NO
I would be much happier if I had my own room.	○ YES	○ NO
My siblings are always in my space.	○ YES	○ NO
I need a bigger bed.	○ YES	○ NO
It would be much better if I had my own bathroom.	○ YES	○ NO
My siblings and I would fight less if we didn't share rooms.	○ YES	○ NO
It's best when I sit in the front seat of the car.	○ YES	○ NO
I would be much better at school if I had a space of my own.	○ YES	○ NO
Our family would be happier in a bigger house.	○ YES	○ NO
We would fight less in a bigger car.	○ YES	○ NO

Did you check yes to any of the statements above? If you did, then you need to work on this area to become more content with the space God has given you. Right now you are believing a big fat lie and you probably don't even realize it.

THE LIE: I need more to fix my problems.

This lie is most often about having more "space" but it truly could be about many things. Somewhere along the way we just start believing that the solution to the problem is to have something different than what we currently have. For example, we truly believe that if we just had our own room, suddenly there would be less fights with our siblings, we would be more effective with our school or homework, and somehow obey our parents more. Do you think this is true?

_____

Let's read Matthew 11:28. Where does Jesus tell us to take our problems? _____

_____

Isn't it wonderful to know that we don't have to solve our problems ourselves? We don't need a bigger room, bigger car, or bigger house in order to get along. We just need God! Do you know how to get God's help when there is a problem? Read Jeremiah 33:3. What do we need to do to get God's help for our problems?

_____
_____
_____
_____

THE TRUTH: God is the answer to our problems.

A Content Heart | ©Not Consumed 2015

Ok, so now we are clear that getting our own space will not help us to be a better sibling, get more schoolwork done, or obey our parents more often. So that means we need a change of attitude about our current "space" situation. Write and/or draw below and share about your space. Describe your room, house, car, etc. Tell all of the things you love about them.

My pastor always has us say, "The problem is me." And it's so true. If we have a problem, chances are there is something we can do about it. Maybe you can't change rooms, can't change your siblings, and can't change the situation, but you can change your attitude. Trust me. This WILL change everything. Can you think of one thing you can do right now to help resolve some of the issues you might have?

___

___

___

PAUSE FOR PRAYER:
Pray and ask God to help you be content with your space. Ask Him to help you be thankful no matter what you have and to do your part to have a good attitude about it.

A Content Heart | ©Not Consumed 2015

My Possessions

Whenever people start talking about becoming more content, they are usually talking about being content with possessions. These are just the things we own, such as a house, car, clothes, toys, electronics, and phones. Below, list 12 things you own.

THINGS I OWN

I think you will easily agree that you have a lot of things, but I'm also certain there are things you want and don't have. Maybe it's a cell phone, a certain style of clothes, or even a toy. Sometimes we can convince ourselves that everyone else besides us has it. When this happens, we become focused on getting that one thing and our hearts don't even notice the big lie that creeps in.

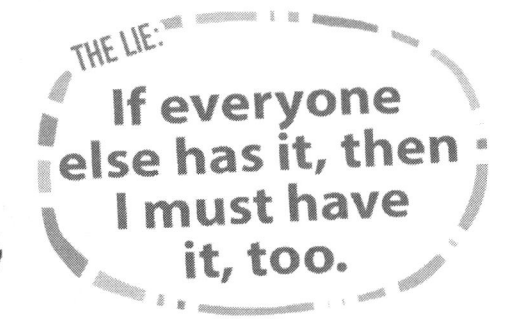

THE LIE: If everyone else has it, then I must have it, too.

This is an easy lie to believe. In fact, we can be quick to make excuses for how this is true. For example, when I was a kid, I tried to convince my mom that if I didn't have designer clothes like other kids, I would be bullied or picked on in school. I wasn't just trying to be happy. I was trying to save my own life! (A bit over-dramatic, don't you think?)

Maybe you have felt this way, too. Let me tell you a secret. Bullies will find something else to pick on if you get those designer clothes. The problem with a bully is THEIR heart, not your lack of possessions. If having something makes you "cool" or more likable it will be a very short-lived and fake friendship. This is not how God wants us to pick our friends.

Look at these verses and remind yourself what real friendship is like.

Proverbs 12:26 _____

Proverbs 13:20 _____

Proverbs 17:17 _____

Let's read one more verse just to be clear on what God says about wanting things that other people have when we don't have them. Look up Exodus 20:17. I don't know about you, but I am not guilty of coveting (wanting) my neighbor's donkey. But I am guilty of the last part. What word or phrase do you see that we are guilty of?

_____

_____

_____

A Content Heart | ©Not Consumed 2015

In case you didn't remember it, this verse is right in the middle of the Ten Commandments. These are laws that God has given us to live by. He didn't say "maybe" or "if it works out for you." God actually commands us to stop wanting things that belong to other people. This doesn't mean that we actually desire to take it away from them. God wants us to protect our hearts against even wanting it to begin with. Remember, we need to be thankful for all that God has given us, not making a list of all that we want Him to give us next.

Read Philippians 4:19 and remind yourself of the truth about how God provides for us. In the box below, write or draw about how God has provided for you. Be sure to include some of your treasured possessions.

THE TRUTH:

God tells us to be content with what He has given us.

PAUSE FOR PRAYER:
So now we have some work to do in our hearts. Are there things that your friends have that you have been wanting? Write them in the space below as you pray and ask God to help you to stop desiring these things and to be thankful for what He has given you.

A Content Heart | ©Not Consumed 2015

My Possessions
(PART 2)

Maybe you aren't too concerned with what your friends have, so coveting their possessions isn't a big problem for you. But that's not the only lie that we believe about our "things." Today we are going to talk about another one. But first, let's take a little quiz to see how you are doing with this one.

When we go to the store, I ask for junk food or treats.	◯ YES	◯ NO
I search on the computer for toys or items I'd like to have.	◯ YES	◯ NO
When the catalog comes, I am the first to circle the things I like.	◯ YES	◯ NO
I can't wait for Christmas, so I can get new things.	◯ YES	◯ NO
My birthday is my favorite day of the year because I love presents.	◯ YES	◯ NO
I leave my toys all over the place.	◯ YES	◯ NO
I have too many toys to play with all of them.	◯ YES	◯ NO

If you answered yes to anything above, you are guilty. But don't be alarmed. All humans are guilty of this to some degree. We all want more than what we have. Sometimes, this desire is a good way to help us become more motivated to work hard. After all, if we didn't need or want things, we might not be as excited about getting our job done.

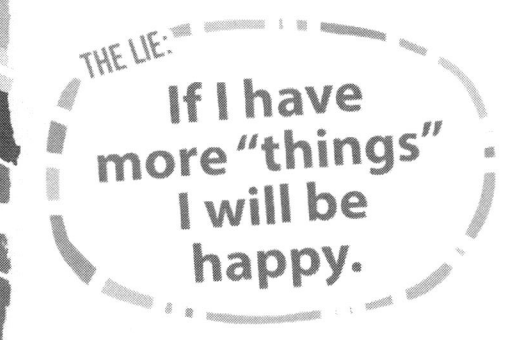

THE LIE: If I have more "things" I will be happy.

But this desire for things can get out of hand very quickly and we give in to a very dangerous lie.

The enemy does a great job of convincing us that we will be so happy as soon as we get that one item we want. We get so focused on getting it that we are willing to do anything to make it happen. Even adults do this. They begin buying things they can't afford and soon find themselves in a heap of credit card debt. Since you are a child, you don't have to worry so much about credit card debt, but you do need to worry about your attitude.

You see, when we become so convinced that we need a certain thing (or things) to make us happy, it becomes very difficult for us to ever get enough. Once we get that first thing, we want something else. Then something else. The cycle keeps right on going, and guess what? We never actually get "happy" even though we get the things we were seeking.

A good example of this can be seen in Hollywood. So many actors and actresses die (or kill themselves) because their lives are so very unhappy. Yet, they are the richest people in the world. They can buy anything they want.... except happiness. Even though they have money, so many of them are completely miserable. You see, no matter how much money you get, you'll never be able to buy happiness.

Do you know why? _____

_____

_____

A Content Heart | ©Not Consumed 2015

Don't worry if you don't know yet. Let's look at some verses that will help us develop a clear biblical answer to this question. Look up each passage below and write anything that helps answer the question.

Proverbs 3:13 _____

Psalm 37:4 _____

Psalm 16:11 _____

Psalm 34:8-10 _____

Using what you learned above, can you tell me why you can't buy happiness or get it by buying more things?

_____

_____

Let's look up Psalm 144:15. For the purposes of the word "happy," look this verse up in the King James Bible. Write the verse below.

_____

_____

THE TRUTH:

Happy are the people whose God is Jehovah.

We know we can't buy happiness with money or things because true happiness comes from knowing God. All of the above verses made that pretty clear, didn't they?

So what do you say we stop making lists of the things we WANT and start making lists of all the things we are thankful for? Wouldn't your next trip to the grocery store be so much more pleasant if you didn't ask for everything you walked by? Perhaps you would enjoy having fewer toys to clean up. Write something you want to change below.

_____

_____

PAUSE FOR PRAYER:
Pray and ask God to help you be happy with the things you have. Ask Him to help you stop desiring more and to find true happiness in your relationship with Him.

A Content Heart | ©Not Consumed 2015

My Gifts

What is your favorite holiday? _____

Why is it your favorite? _____
_____
_____

THE LIE: Holidays are for getting.

Most kids will answer that question with something about gifts. Perhaps they love Christmas or their birthday because they love getting gifts. Are you one of those kids? _____

Getting a gift is a wonderful thing. People who love us often enjoy giving us gifts and we should enjoy getting them just as much. The trouble is, sometimes we get caught up in yet another dangerous lie.

In the box below draw the best gift you've ever gotten.

What are some words that describe this gift?

Have you ever stopped to think about why people give gifts? Why do we give gifts for Christmas, birthdays, or any other time of the year? Usually, we give gifts to the people we love: our family, friends, maybe even teachers. We give the gifts because we want to express this love to others. All of this is a good thing, but when it takes over our heart, it's not so good.

Have you ever thought about the real meaning of Christmas? What is it? _____
_____
_____

A Content Heart | ©Not Consumed 2015

Whether it's Easter, Christmas, or even a birthday, the holidays are NOT for getting. The purpose is to spend time as a family, thank God for the gifts He has given us, and to give graciously to others in return.

Yes, I just said that you are supposed to be GIVING at Christmas, not getting. I'm not saying it's wrong to get a gift from someone, but our attitude in the process can be very wrong. Let me show you what I mean. Circle any of the things that are true below.

> **THE TRUTH:**
> **The holidays are for giving.**

- I make long wish lists before a holiday of the gifts I'd like to have.
- If someone gives me a gift that I don't like, I'm annoyed or even rude.
- I spend a lot of time guessing and wondering what people will buy me.
- I ask people to buy things for me.

I'm sorry to tell you this, but all of the attitudes above are wrong. Do any of them sound like thoughts that will help you understand the true meaning of a holiday? Are any of those attitudes focused on giving to others?

This is probably the hardest lesson to learn. Our world is completely upside down. Christmas has become a festival of greed, demanding that kids beg for more and more every year. Don't be that kid. Be different. But don't feel like this means you will be missing out.

Read Acts 20:35 and Luke 6:38. If you focus on giving, what do these verses promise?

_____

_____

_____

And besides, if you are a Christian, you already have the greatest gift of all. What is it? (Hint: see John 3:16)

_____

PAUSE FOR PRAYER:
Pray and ask God to help you to focus your thoughts on giving instead of getting when it comes to holidays. Ask Him to help you find someone that you can bless with time, gifts, or even food. Ask Him to help you to be truly thankful for any gift that is given to you.

A Content Heart | ©Not Consumed 2015

Review

A CONTENT HEART **A CONTENT HEART** **A CONTENT HEART**

PRACTICE THE TRUTH:

We hear the lies of the world every day. In fact, they are so common in our culture that we don't even realize we are hearing them. We must fight these lies by rehearsing or practicing the truth out loud to ourselves. Fill in the blanks and write these truths. Then practice saying them out loud 3 times.

THE TRUTH: God is the answer to our problems.

THE TRUTH: God tells us to be content with what He has given us.

15 THINGS I'M THANKFUL FOR RIGHT NOW

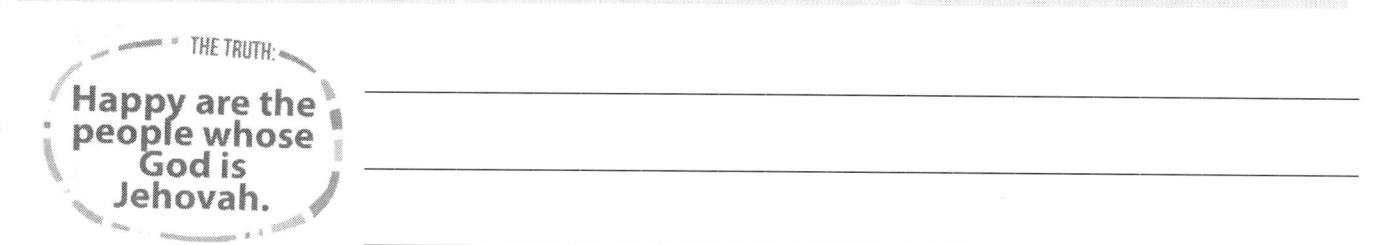

THE TRUTH: Happy are the people whose God is Jehovah.

DRAW THREE THINGS YOU DON'T NEED TO BE HAPPY.

A Content Heart | ©Not Consumed 2015

THE TRUTH: The holidays are for giving.

What is the next holiday coming up? _____
Make a plan for how you will give to others. Circle the ideas you like or write in some new ones of your own.

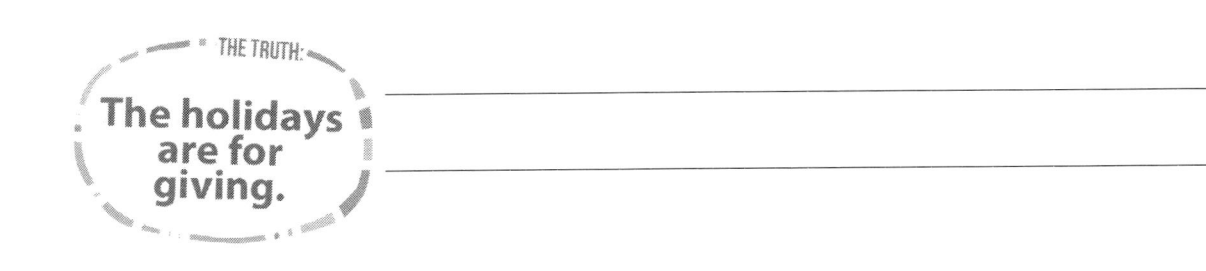

Take dinner or groceries to a family in need.
Hold open the door.
Give a few dollars to a homeless person.
Write a kind note.
Read a book to someone.
Help your parents.
Set the table.
Put a note in someone's lunch.

Volunteer in a soup kitchen.
Return a cart for someone.
Let someone go first.
Weed or shovel for a neighbor.
Bake a homemade treat.
Help a sibling clean up.
Pick up something that was dropped.
Bring a candy bar for a friend or teacher.

It's hard to believe we've come so far in the last few weeks. Have you seen a change in your heart? Write about what you have learned the most.

What are three things you can do right away to continue to be more content every day of your life?

I'm praying for you and cheering you on. Don't forget to ask your parents to pray for you as you continue to grow to be more content. And of course, ask God to help you each and every day!

A Content Heart | ©Not Consumed 2015

Made in the USA
Charleston, SC
27 September 2016